WHEN GOD OPENS THE DOOR

31 Day Devotional of God's Favor

Nate Freeman

CONTENTS

INTRODUCTION

Living in the Rythm of Favor

You didn't stumble onto this book by accident. Favor brought you here. It might not look like it, and it might not feel like it, but even in the middle of your mess, God's fingerprints are all over your story. You are in the rhythm of favor—even if the beat feels off right now.

Favor isn't a fairytale, a prosperity pitch, or some spiritual lottery ticket. It's the evidence of God's intentional hand on your life. It's when heaven interrupts the ordinary. When doors open that you didn't knock on. When resources show up that you didn't qualify for. When peace floods your heart before the answer even comes. Favor is God going before you, working behind the scenes, and staying with you every step of the way.

Too many people think favor is about living easy,

but if that were true, Jesus—the most favored One—would've lived a life without pain. Instead, He was born in obscurity, misunderstood by the masses, rejected by the religious, and crucified by the crowd. Yet in all that, He never lost favor—He fulfilled it. Favor isn't the absence of struggle; it's the assurance of presence.

This 31-day journey isn't just devotional. It's a prophetic activation. Every chapter is a seed. And the soil? Your heart. If you let this word get in you—not just in your ears, but deep down in your spirit—you'll begin to see life differently. You'll stop asking, "Why me?" and start declaring, "Why not me?" Because favor doesn't skip those with a past. Favor doesn't avoid people who've failed. Favor finds the faithful, the available, and the surrendered.

And hear me—favor is not random. It's strategic. It's surgical. It's sacred. You don't earn it. You don't deserve it. But when God releases it, nothing can stop it. Not people. Not systems. Not even you.

You might be in a valley right now, or standing on a mountaintop. You might be in transition, wondering what's next. Or maybe you're just trying to make it through the day. Wherever you are, I want you to remember this:

Favor doesn't chase feelings. It follows purpose.

This book is your invitation to shift from striving to receiving, from surviving to thriving, from wandering to walking in divine alignment. With each day, you'll hear stories of unlikely people touched by unexplainable grace—just like you. You'll see how God used fields, pits, prisons, palaces, and even trees to showcase His favor. And by the end of this journey, I believe you'll be able to look at your life—not just the highs, but the lows—and say with boldness:

"Surely, goodness and favor have been following me all along."

CHAPTER 1: FAVOR, NOT FORTUNE

There's a moment in Joseph's story that doesn't get enough credit. It's not the robe. It's not the pit. It's not even the palace. It's the moment Pharaoh looks at a former prisoner, a Hebrew with no political clout, and says, "You're in charge now." That's not hustle. That's favor.

Let's be honest—if we're judging by credentials, Joseph didn't belong in that room. He didn't climb the corporate ladder. He didn't pad his résumé. He just kept showing up, faithful in places most people would've checked out. And that's what makes favor so disruptive. It doesn't follow the rules. It rewrites them.

You see, the world will tell you that fortune comes to

those who grind the hardest, network the smartest, and keep their image flawless. But favor? Favor doesn't need filters. It finds you in prison clothes and pulls you into places of power. It's not random —it's sovereign. It's God saying, "I see you. I choose you. And I'm placing you where you never thought you'd stand."

Genesis 41:41–42 gives us the scene: Pharaoh takes off his signet ring and places it on Joseph's hand. That ring didn't just represent authority—it was authority. It meant Joseph could speak on the king's behalf. Think about that. One moment, Joseph is forgotten. The next, he's second in command. That's not a lucky break. That's divine reversal.

Here's the truth: Favor doesn't always feel like favor. Sometimes it looks like betrayal. Like being lied on. Like being passed over. Sometimes favor disguises itself in struggle because God is not just positioning you—He's preparing you. Before Joseph ever stepped into Pharaoh's courts, he learned integrity in Potiphar's house and endurance in prison. His character was catching up to his calling.

And maybe that's where you are right now. You're wondering why the promotion hasn't come. Why the relationship didn't work. Why the door won't open. But what if the delay is not denial—what if it's development? What if God is building something in you before He builds something through you?

See, we love the idea of favor when it comes with

increase. But favor is more than abundance. It's alignment. It's being in the right place at the right time with the right posture. And sometimes that place doesn't feel right at all—until God breathes on it.

Let me speak to that part of you that's discouraged: you're not overlooked. You're hidden on purpose. God's not punishing you—He's preserving you. Because when favor hits, it's going to move so fast you'll look back and realize this—yes, even this—was part of the plan all along.

Joseph didn't chase the throne. He stewarded the assignment. And when the time was right, the throne found him. That's what favor does. It doesn't respond to striving. It responds to faithfulness.

So here's your call today: Stop trying to manufacture what only God can release. Stop trying to prove you're ready and just be ready. Your name is already in conversations you know nothing about. Your moment is already on heaven's calendar. All God needs is your consistency in the in-between.

You may not have the platform. You may not have the pedigree. But you've got the presence of God —and that's enough. Because favor doesn't need fortune to flow. Favor is the fortune.

Remember this: what looks like a delay is often God setting the stage for destiny. Don't flinch. Don't fold. Just keep moving. You don't have to fight your way in when God is about to call you forward.

Scripture Focus:

"See, I have placed you over all the land of Egypt." — Genesis 41:41 (NASB 1995)

Reflection Question:

Are you trying to force a door open that favor hasn't unlocked yet?

Declaration:

I don't chase favor—I carry it. And in God's time, I will be exactly where I'm supposed to be.

CHAPTER 2: REDIRECTION IS STILL FAVOR

We've all been there—waiting for the phone call, hoping for the opportunity, praying that this time will be different. And then comes the rejection. The silence. The closed door that slams so hard it rattles your confidence. But here's the thing most people don't realize: sometimes, favor says no because God is making room for a better yes.

In 1 Samuel 16:1, God speaks to Samuel:

"How long will you mourn for Saul, since I have rejected him from being king over Israel? Fill your horn with oil and go; I will send you to Jesse the Bethlehemite, for I have selected a king for Myself among his sons."

Now imagine that. Samuel is grieving over what used to be. Saul was Israel's first king. He looked the part. He was the part—at least for a while. But the season shifted, and Samuel's oil was stuck in yesterday. God had already moved on, but Samuel hadn't caught up yet.

That's what happens to many of us. We mourn closed doors like they're failures when really, they're divine redirections. Favor isn't always about stepping into something—it's also about stepping away from what no longer fits. What looks like rejection is often protection. God will remove you from rooms that can't hold your future and relationships that can't carry your calling.

Favor doesn't mean every door will swing wide open. Sometimes it means the door stays shut because what's behind it would've destroyed you. Favor doesn't just elevate—it insulates. God's no is just as powerful as His yes.

Let me break it down. You might be upset about a missed opportunity, but what if that "missed" opportunity would've locked you into mediocrity? What if God's silence in one season is Him rerouting you toward something so much greater?

That job you didn't get? That relationship that didn't work? That platform that overlooked you? It wasn't rejection. It was redirection. And redirection is still favor.

You are not behind. You are not forgotten. God's favor doesn't always take the shortest route, but it always takes the surest one. The oil was never meant to stay with Saul. It was meant to flow over David. And your oil—your calling, your gifts, your anointing—it's not wasted. It's waiting for the right assignment.

Here's what I've learned in my own life: when I stopped chasing what was gone, I started receiving what was coming. You can't walk into God's next while holding onto yesterday's "almost."

Maybe you've been sitting in a season like Samuel, mourning a door that closed, questioning your worth, your timing, your direction. Let me speak this to your spirit: "Fill your horn with oil and go." In other words, get ready again. Pack your faith. God's about to reveal what the last "no" was really making space for.

You won't always understand the process, but favor doesn't require understanding—only trust. You don't have to see the whole path to take the next step. God's favor often feels backwards before it moves forward. But He's still working. Still weaving. Still writing your story.

And hear me—it's not over. The best doors haven't opened yet. The right people haven't found you yet. The most strategic timing hasn't arrived yet. But it's coming. Keep your horn full and your heart expectant.

Scripture Focus:

"I have selected a king for Myself among his sons." — 1 Samuel 16:1 (NASB 1995)

Reflection Question:

What are you still mourning that God has already moved past?

Declaration:

God's redirection is not rejection. It's preparation. I trust Him to lead me into the right season, with the right people, at the right time.

CHAPTER 3: OVERFLOW IN OBEDIENCE

L et's talk about what happens when you're doing everything right—and still coming up empty. You're clocking in, showing up, praying hard, giving faithfully... and nothing seems to shift. The nets stay dry. The breakthrough feels delayed. And heaven? Quiet.

That's exactly where we find Peter in Luke 5.

He wasn't being lazy. He wasn't ignoring his calling. He was doing what he knew to do. Fishing—his livelihood—was how he provided. And yet, Scripture tells us he had toiled all night and caught nothing.

That's a word right there: toiled. Some of us know what it's like to toil. It's not just work—it's weariness. It's pouring yourself out and seeing no return. It's the kind of tired that sleep can't fix. And for Peter, after a night of fruitless effort, the last thing he expected was favor.

But then, Jesus shows up.

He steps into Peter's boat—not after the catch, but before it. Before the abundance. Before the overflow. Before the success. Jesus always arrives before the outcome, because favor isn't a reward for results—it's a response to obedience.

Jesus tells Peter, "Launch out into the deep and let down your nets for a catch."

Let me modernize that: "Try again. Go deeper. I know it didn't work before, but this time, I'm in it."

Now here's the tension. Peter could've easily said no. He could've said, "Jesus, I'm the fisherman here. I've got years of experience. You're a carpenter, a teacher—this isn't your lane." But instead, Peter says something that unlocks everything:

"Nevertheless, at Your word..."

That right there is where favor flips the story.

"Nevertheless" is the language of the faithful. It's what you say when your logic doesn't line up, but your spirit still leans in. It's the bridge between exhaustion and expectation. Peter obeyed—not because it made sense, but because the Word said so. And as soon as he did, the nets overflowed to the point of breaking.

That's what favor does. It turns empty nets into sinking boats.

You don't need a new net—you need a fresh yes.

You don't need a new sea—you need a deeper obedience.

God is not waiting on better conditions—He's waiting on bolder trust.

Too often, we want favor to follow convenience. We want the blessing without the obedience, the overflow without the launch. But God doesn't bless what you intend to do. He blesses what you step out and do—especially when it costs you comfort.

And notice this: the miracle didn't happen when Peter was casting for himself. It happened when Jesus borrowed his boat. Favor flows through surrendered spaces. The moment you give God your business, your platform, your plan—He multiplies what's left in your hand.

What if your obedience is the very thing holding back your overflow?

What if one act of faith is all that stands between where you are and where God is trying to take you?

I believe there are some people reading this who've been rowing in circles. You're tired. You're disillusioned. You're questioning whether it's even worth it to keep pushing. And here's what I hear the Spirit of God saying: "Launch again. This time, I'm in it."

Favor doesn't erase fatigue—but it makes the effort worth it. Favor doesn't promise ease—but it guarantees impact.

Let your "nevertheless" be louder than your "I'm tired."

Because this time, the nets won't just hold fish —they'll hold evidence. Evidence that when Jesus steps into your situation, empty doesn't stand a chance.

Scripture Focus:

"When they had done this, they enclosed a great quantity of fish, and their nets began to break." — Luke 5:6 (NASB 1995)

Reflection Question:

What area of your life is God asking you to launch again in obedience?

Declaration:

I may be tired, but I'm still obedient. I'm launching again—not in my strength, but with Jesus in my boat. Favor is in the deep.

CHAPTER 4: TRIMMED FOR TRIUMPH

Sometimes favor doesn't look like a blessing. It looks like subtraction. Like God is taking things away right when you feel like you need them most. People leave. Resources dry up. Plans unravel. And you're left staring at a smaller team, a thinner bank account, or a stripped-down version of what you thought it would take to win.

That's exactly where Gideon stood.

He started with 32,000 soldiers. That's a solid army—strong enough to feel confident, maybe even secure. But God wasn't interested in comfort. He was after clarity. He told Gideon, "You have too many." Imagine that—too many people to fulfill the promise. Too much strength for God to get the glory.

So He starts cutting.

First 22,000 leave out of fear. Then another 9,700 are dismissed based on how they drink water. And Gideon is left with 300. From 32,000 down to 300. From plenty to barely enough. From strong odds to impossible ones.

But here's the twist: God didn't reduce Gideon's army to punish him. He reduced it to prove Him.

Because favor doesn't need numbers—favor needs trust.

We often think we need more to do more. But in the kingdom, less with God always outweighs more without Him. God will trim your circle, your strategy, even your options—not to set you up for failure, but to set the stage for a victory so undeniable, only He could've done it.

Let me speak to the person who's been losing more than they're gaining lately. You've watched people walk away. You've lost connections you thought were critical. You've felt God remove some crutches you were leaning on. And it feels like you're going backward.

But hear me: You are not being buried—you're being positioned.

Sometimes God has to take it away so you stop trusting it. The numbers were never your strength. The people were never your source. The plan was never your protection. He is. And when favor is on your life, it will strip the scaffolding so you can finally see the structure He's building in you.

Favor doesn't make you flashy. It makes you focused.

Gideon didn't win with quantity. He won with clarity. He knew who was with him, and more importantly, Who was behind him. And when God is behind you, the odds don't matter. The 300 weren't the reason they won—the obedience was.

Let's get practical. What has God trimmed in your life lately? What looks like loss but might actually be grace? Could it be that the relationship that didn't last was God making space for one that will? Could the closed door have protected you from walking into a counterfeit?

Here's a truth I've lived: God will reduce your resources to reveal His reliability. When all you have left is Him, you find out He's all you ever needed.

You may not have the army you once had. But you've got favor. And favor with 300 is better than fear with 32,000.

God's not trying to humiliate you. He's trying to highlight you—so that when the victory comes, no one can say it was by your own hand.

So stand in that smaller space with bigger faith. Lift your head, even if your hands feel empty. Because what God is about to do through your less will blow your mind—and silence every doubt.

Scripture Focus:

"The Lord said to Gideon, 'With the 300 men who lapped I will deliver you and give the Midianites into your hands.'" — Judges 7:7 (NASB 1995)

Reflection Question:

What is God trimming in your life that you've been calling a loss?

Declaration:

I will not fear the reduction. God is refining my resources to reveal His favor. Victory is coming, and He alone will get the glory.

CHAPTER 5:
STRENGTH FOR
THE CLIMB

Y ou've prayed. You've cried. You've fasted. You've done everything you know how to do —and the mountain still won't move. And now you're wondering... Where's the favor in that?

We tend to think of favor as a detour around difficulty. But sometimes, favor doesn't remove the mountain—it gives you the strength to climb it. That's not the version of favor we ask for, but it's often the one we need most.

Paul understood this tension. In 2 Corinthians 12, he talks about a "thorn in the flesh"—something painful, persistent, and completely out of his control. He pleaded with God three times to take it away. And if anyone had favor, it was Paul. He was planting churches, writing scripture, shaking kingdoms. Surely God would honor that kind of service with a miracle, right?

But the answer wasn't removal. It was revelation.

"My grace is sufficient for you, for power is perfected in weakness."

— 2 Corinthians 12:9

That wasn't a dismissal. It was a divine strategy.

Favor didn't take away Paul's pain. It taught him how to walk with it—and still win.

Because hear me: Favor doesn't always show up in the form of escape. Sometimes it shows up as endurance.

We don't like that kind of favor. We'd rather it fix everything fast. But if favor only showed up when life was easy, it wouldn't mean much. Real favor sustains you when nothing else can. It keeps you standing when others fold. It pushes you forward when your strength is gone. Favor is not always the removal of the struggle—it's the reason you're still standing in the middle of it.

Sometimes the mountain stays. The thorn stays. The prayer goes unanswered. And yet—you keep moving. That's favor.

You don't always need God to lighten the load. Sometimes you need Him to strengthen your back. And when He does? That's when you realize that favor isn't just something you wear—it's something you walk in.

And here's what I've come to know personally: Some of God's greatest moves in my life came not when He took something away, but when He gave me the grace to carry it.

Favor doesn't keep you from pain—it keeps you from being defined by it.

You may be carrying grief, pressure, uncertainty, illness, or fear. And the enemy would love to convince you that God's silence is absence. But it's not. It's strategy. Because when you make it with the thorn, when you climb with the weight, when you praise with the ache—that's when people start asking, "How are you still standing?"

And your answer? "Grace."

Not your strength. Not your plan. Not your performance. Just grace. Favor has a sound, and it often sounds like a whisper in the dark: "Keep going. I'm with you."

So here's my encouragement to you today: Stop waiting for the mountain to move. Start climbing. Not because you're strong, but because He is. And every step you take is proof that favor doesn't fail—it just works differently than we expected.

Scripture Focus:

"My grace is sufficient for you, for power is perfected in weakness." — 2 Corinthians 12:9 (NASB 1995)

Reflection Question:

Where have you been asking God for removal when He might be offering you strength instead?

Declaration:

I don't need the mountain to move—I need the strength to climb. His grace is carrying me, and His favor is enough.

CHAPTER 6:
CLEARED FOR CONNECTION

L et's be real—favor can get lonely.

No one tells you that, do they? That sometimes, God's favor on your life won't attract people. It'll expose them. It'll reveal who was only walking with you for what you had, not who you are. It'll shift your circle and stir your atmosphere. And if you're not careful, you'll mistake divine disconnection for personal rejection.

That's exactly what happened with Jesus.

In John 6, He's been performing miracles, feeding thousands, speaking truth. The crowds are swelling. The buzz is growing. But then He starts teaching things that don't feel good. That challenge comfort. That call people deeper. And suddenly, the same crowd that was celebrating Him starts backing away.

"From that time many of His disciples went back and walked with Him no more."

—John 6:66

Did you catch that? They walked with Him no more. Not because He failed. Not because He changed. But because favor stopped being convenient for them.

Jesus turns to the twelve and asks a question that echoes across every generation of the called:

"Do you also want to go away?"

—John 6:67

See, sometimes favor will make people uncomfortable. Because when God starts elevating you, stretching you, calling you into more—it reminds people of what they've settled for. And instead of celebrating your favor, they withdraw from your future. That's not your fault. That's divine pruning.

Favor doesn't just bring blessings—it brings clarity. It cleans your room, not to punish you, but to prepare you. God will let people walk away so you can walk into what's next.

I know—it hurts. It's confusing. We ask questions like, "Why did they leave?" or "What did I do wrong?" But the truth is, some exits are orchestrated. Some subtractions are sacred. And some goodbyes are God making room for the right "yes."

Here's what I've learned in my own life:

The presence of favor will always create a fork in the road. Some will stay. Some will go. And both are a blessing.

When God calls you higher, He doesn't ask for a vote. He invites you into a new level of trust. And at that level, not everyone can walk with you. Some people are attached to the version of you that stayed small. Some are loyal to your potential only when it benefits them. But when favor grows loud, the fake gets quiet.

And it's okay.

Because favor doesn't isolate you—it insulates you. God will clear the room so you can hear His voice more clearly. He'll reduce the noise so you stop questioning your worth. And He'll strengthen your core team—not by adding more bodies, but by revealing who's really for you.

Look at what Peter says in the very next verse:

"Lord, to whom shall we go? You have words of eternal life."

—John 6:68

Now that's favor—having even just one person who stays because they're connected to your calling, not just your comfort.

So if you're in a season of subtraction, take heart. This isn't the enemy stealing from you—it's God streamlining you. He's cutting weight, clarifying motives, and setting the stage. Because where you're going, loyalty matters more than numbers.

Don't mourn the ones who left. Celebrate the One who stayed. His name is Jesus. And if He hasn't walked away, neither should you.

Scripture Focus:

"You do not want to go away also, do you?" — John 6:67 (NASB 1995)

Reflection Question:

Who left your life that God might have removed for your protection?

Declaration:

I will not chase what God has released. Favor makes room by removing what can't grow with me. I am surrounded by exactly who I need for what's next.

CHAPTER 7:
EYES ON THE
WINDWALKER

The storm was real. The waves were loud. The wind wasn't playing games. And yet, in the middle of all that chaos, Peter did something outrageous—he stepped out of the boat.

Let's pause there. That's favor. Not the absence of the storm, but the presence of Jesus in it. Favor doesn't always still the storm before you step. Sometimes it invites you into the storm to prove the storm doesn't control your story.

Peter walks on water. You know the moment. He's defying gravity, defying logic, defying fear. And for a moment, his feet are on waves and his eyes are locked on Jesus. But then—something shifts.

"But seeing the wind, he became frightened, and

when he began to sink, he cried out, 'Lord, save me!'"

— Matthew 14:30 (NASB 1995)

Peter didn't sink because the storm got worse. He sank because he changed his focus.

Favor doesn't remove the wind—it trains your eyes.

Let that settle. The moment Peter looked at what was happening around him instead of Who was standing in front of him, fear took over. It's the same with us. Favor gives us access to walk on things that used to drown us—but the enemy knows, if he can get your focus, he can take your footing.

The storm isn't your problem—your sight is.

When you stop looking at Jesus, you start leaning into fear. You start calculating the risk, rehearsing the worst-case scenario, comparing yourself to people who never left the boat. You start drowning not because you lack favor—but because you let fear reinterpret it.

But I love what happens next. Peter cries out, "Lord, save me!" And Jesus doesn't scold him. He doesn't let him sink to prove a point. He immediately reaches out His hand.

That's favor.

Favor is not the absence of sinking moments—it's the certainty that even when you start to go under, grace will grab you. Favor doesn't mean you'll never wobble. It means when you do, Jesus is close enough to catch you.

And that's where some of us are today. We stepped out. We started the business. We said yes to the call. We trusted God in the deep. But somewhere between faith and fulfillment, the storm got louder, and we started sinking.

Here's your reminder: The same Jesus who called you out of the boat is still standing on the water. He hasn't moved. You're still favored.

Don't let the storm make you forget the invitation. Jesus didn't say, "Peter, come," just to watch him fail. He knew the storm would test him—but He also knew the moment would grow him.

And maybe that's the purpose of this season. Not to crush you. Not to drown you. But to teach you how to walk with your eyes on the Windwalker.

Because favor isn't about perfection—it's about direction. Every time you shift your focus back to Him, favor pulls you up. Every time you call out His name, grace comes rushing in.

You may have gotten distracted. You may feel like you're going under. But it's not over.

The miracle didn't end with the first step. It continued the moment Peter reached up—and Jesus pulled him back.

Scripture Focus:

"But seeing the wind, he became frightened, and when he began to sink, he cried out, 'Lord, save me!'"
— Matthew 14:30 (NASB 1995)

Reflection Question:

What's stealing your focus from Jesus in this season?

Declaration:

I fix my eyes on the One who called me. Storms may rise, but favor holds me steady. Even when I sink, grace will lift me.

CHAPTER 8:
FAVOR MAKES
A WAY

Y ou've been doing everything right—walking in obedience, following the cloud, trusting God step by step—and then suddenly, you hit a wall. A Red Sea. An immovable, impassable, impossible barrier. And just to add pressure, the enemy is closing in behind you.

That's where the Israelites were in Exodus 14. They had finally broken free from Egypt after 400 years of slavery. They didn't run away—they were led out. This was God's doing. So you'd think the path would be clear. But instead, He leads them straight to a dead end.

No boats. No bridges. Just water in front and war behind.

And yet, this is favor.

Because favor isn't just about open doors—it's about divine detours that reveal God's glory in ways you never saw coming.

Exodus 14:21 says:

"Then Moses stretched out his hand over the sea; and the Lord swept the sea back by a strong east wind all night, and turned the sea into dry land, so the waters were divided."

Let that sink in: all night.

We picture the miracle happening in a flash—but it didn't. God sent a wind that worked through the night. While they were terrified. While they were questioning. While they were ready to turn back— God was working in the dark.

That's favor.

Sometimes favor doesn't feel like light and celebration. Sometimes it's wind and waves and waiting. Sometimes it's midnight and you don't see any change—but something is shifting beneath the surface.

Favor doesn't always look like a breakthrough at first. Sometimes it looks like a long night and a strong wind.

And here's what's powerful: the sea didn't disappear. God didn't airlift them over it. He split it. In other words, He didn't remove the obstacle—He transformed it.

God's favor won't always eliminate the problem, but it will make a path through it.

We often want God to take us around the pain, around the struggle, around the fight. But real favor walks you through what others drown in. The same waters that looked like death became the passage to their deliverance.

What if the thing standing in front of you isn't your ending—but the stage for your miracle?

What if the pressure you're feeling isn't punishment —but proof that God's about to move in a way that defies logic?

Because here's the truth: favor doesn't mean you won't face opposition. It means opposition can't stop what God has already ordained. He didn't bring you this far to abandon you at the water's edge.

So if it feels like you're boxed in—like there's no way forward and too much behind you to turn back—lift your eyes. Lift your faith. Because even in the dark, even in the chaos, God is still making a way.

The winds are already blowing. The seas are already shifting. Favor is already clearing a path you can't see yet.

All God needs is your faith to stretch out like Moses' hand—believing that dry ground is coming.

Scripture Focus:

"Then Moses stretched out his hand over the sea; and the Lord swept the sea back by a strong east wind all night, and turned the sea into dry land, so the waters were divided." — Exodus 14:21 (NASB 1995)

Reflection Question:

Where in your life does it feel like you're facing a dead end that God may actually be preparing to split?

Declaration:

I may not see the way, but I trust the One who makes it. Even in the dark, favor is working. God is parting the waters for me.

CHAPTER 9:
THE WAIT IS
NOT A WASTE

W aiting can feel like the worst kind of wilderness. You're anointed, but not yet appointed. Called, but not yet crowned. You know there's more in you, but nothing around you looks like what God promised. It's the space between prophecy and fulfillment—and it can mess with your mind if you let it.

That's where David was.

In 1 Samuel 16:13, the prophet Samuel anoints David in front of his brothers. Oil pours. Destiny is declared. Favor falls. And what does David do next?

He goes back to tending sheep.

Let that settle in. He wasn't handed a throne.

He wasn't moved into the palace. He wasn't even invited to stay at the prophet's side. The oil flowed—but his surroundings stayed the same.

"Then Samuel took the horn of oil and anointed him in the midst of his brothers; and the Spirit of the Lord came mightily upon David from that day forward."

— 1 Samuel 16:13 (NASB 1995)

From that day forward, David was chosen. But it took years before he sat on the throne God promised. And in those years—those long, quiet, tension-filled years—David didn't chase the crown. He grew into it.

Because favor doesn't fast-track you. It forms you.

That's the part we don't like. We want instant elevation. Immediate recognition. Microwave miracles. But God isn't building a moment—He's building a man, a woman, a legacy. And that takes time.

The wait is not a punishment. It's preparation.

You see, the same hands that slayed giants were first trained by defending sheep. The same voice that led a nation first learned to worship in obscurity. God used isolation to shape David's character so that when elevation came, his heart could carry the weight of the crown.

And I need to tell somebody reading this: God is not

stalling—He's strengthening.

Don't mistake silence for absence. Don't confuse stillness with stagnation. Favor doesn't just show up when you arrive—it's active while you're becoming. And the field you've been frustrated in? That's where your skills are sharpening. That's where your intimacy with God is deepening. That's where your identity is being sealed.

Let's be honest. Waiting hurts. Watching others get their moment while you stay in the shadows? It can feel personal. But hear me: when you're favored, you don't have to force anything. When it's your time, the throne will come looking for you.

God isn't just timing your promotion—He's timing your protection.

If David had been promoted too soon, he would've entered a system not yet ready to receive him. Sometimes God delays you to preserve what's pure in you.

And that's where trust comes in. Trust that the oil wasn't wasted. Trust that what was declared over you will manifest. Trust that the same God who called you is also keeping you—even when the crown feels far away.

You might still be in the pasture. You might still feel unseen. But the anointing is already on you. You're not waiting for favor—you're walking in it. The waiting is part of the favor.

Because when the moment comes, you won't just step into the role—you'll be ready for it.

Scripture Focus:

"Then Samuel took the horn of oil and anointed him in the midst of his brothers; and the Spirit of the Lord came mightily upon David from that day forward." — 1 Samuel 16:13 (NASB 1995)

Reflection Question:

Are you despising your field season instead of recognizing it as God's training ground?

Declaration:

I am not forgotten. I am being formed. The wait is not a waste—God's favor is preparing me for what's already mine.

CHAPTER 10:
KEEP BUILDING
IN THE RAIN

Sometimes favor doesn't feel like a flood of blessings—it feels like the flood hasn't come yet, and all you've got is a hammer, a word, and a whole lot of questions.

That's Noah's story.

God told him to build an ark... before there was a single drop of rain. No thunderclouds, no forecast, no sign in the sky. Just an assignment. "Build." And he obeyed.

"Make for yourself an ark of gopher wood; you shall make the ark with rooms, and shall cover it inside and out with pitch."

— Genesis 6:14 (NASB 1995)

Noah built for years. Hammered when people laughed. Measured when no one understood. Sawed and nailed while critics rolled their eyes and culture called him crazy. And through it all, he held onto one thing: God's instruction was enough.

Favor doesn't always look like applause. Sometimes it looks like isolation. It looks like holding a vision no one else can see and choosing to build anyway. That's favor—not because of how others respond, but because of how God is directing.

You see, favor doesn't shield you from the work—it empowers you to finish it.

God gave Noah the dimensions, the materials, and the blueprint, but He didn't give him a weather report. That's because favor doesn't follow confirmation—it creates it. You don't need five signs when you've got a Word. And if God said build, build —even if no one else brings their tools.

Let's talk about the discipline of preparation. Noah prepared in a season that didn't look like it needed preparation. He built something for a future no one else believed in. That's the tension of favor—it invites you to obey before you understand.

Some of you are in that place right now. You're building a business, writing a book, raising kids, showing up at a job, serving faithfully in ministry —and it feels like no one sees, nothing's happening, and you're stuck in pre-rain obedience.

Don't stop building.

Because here's the key: The flood didn't validate the ark—the obedience did.

The storm didn't make Noah right. His faithfulness did. And when the rain finally came, the one who looked foolish for years became the one whose favor made a way for survival.

God's favor will make you build things that don't make sense—until they do. And when it all starts coming together, you won't have to explain yourself. The rain will speak for you.

Sometimes the flood is not your problem—it's your proof. And when it comes, you'll be ready—not because you rushed, but because you obeyed.

God never wastes obedience. Every swing of the hammer, every inch of wood, every act of preparation—it matters.

And don't miss this: Noah didn't just build for himself. His obedience saved his family. That's how favor works—it blesses through you. It covers more than just you. Your obedience today might be the ark that carries someone else through their storm tomorrow.

So don't let delay stop your discipline. Don't let the absence of evidence cancel your assignment. Keep showing up. Keep measuring, sawing, trusting. Favor is in the faithfulness, not just the flood.

The rain is coming—but what matters most is that your hands stay on the work God gave you.

Scripture Focus:

"Make for yourself an ark of gopher wood; you shall make the ark with rooms, and shall cover it inside and out with pitch." — Genesis 6:14 (NASB 1995)

Reflection Question:

Where have you paused your building because the rain hasn't come yet?

Declaration:

I will build by faith, not by forecast. Even when I don't see the rain, I trust the assignment. Favor is in my obedience.

CHAPTER 11: DOUBLE FOR THE DAMAGE

There are moments in life that break more than your heart—they break your rhythm. You're walking in favor, trusting God, doing your best to stay faithful... and then life hits. Unexpected. Unfair. Unrelenting. And you start asking the same question Job must've asked a thousand times: "Why me?"

Job didn't lose a little—he lost everything. His children. His wealth. His health. His reputation. All gone. And to make it worse, he was surrounded by voices that tried to explain his suffering like it was somehow his fault. But the truth was deeper. Job's life wasn't about punishment—it was about purpose. And favor was still at work, even in the ashes.

"The Lord restored the fortunes of Job when he prayed for his friends, and the Lord increased all that Job had twofold."

— Job 42:10 (NASB 1995)

Double.

That's not compensation. That's restoration with interest. That's God saying, "I saw the tears. I heard the groans. I counted the losses. And now, I'm paying it back—with favor."

Let's be clear: favor doesn't prevent suffering. But it redeems it.

Job's restoration didn't begin when he got all the answers. It began when he let go of the offense and interceded for the very people who misunderstood him. That's not weakness. That's maturity. That's favor making you better instead of bitter.

You see, the enemy's strategy wasn't just to take Job's stuff. It was to fracture his faith. To poison his heart. To convince him that the pain proved God had left him. But favor was never absent. It was just buried under the wreckage—waiting to resurrect something deeper.

Sometimes favor isn't loud. It's quiet. It sits with you in the dust. It holds your breathless prayers. It waits until the moment your heart is soft enough to bless those who hurt you. Then it moves.

Let me ask you something: What if your recovery

isn't waiting on your circumstances—it's waiting on your release?

Job's breakthrough was tied to his forgiveness. When he prayed for his friends, favor flowed. That's not just theology—that's principle. Favor flows where freedom lives. And sometimes, freedom looks like blessing the very ones who doubted you while you were bleeding.

God didn't give Job back the exact same things—He gave him better. That's how favor operates. It doesn't just rewind. It rebuilds. And what comes after the fire is stronger, deeper, richer.

I know what it's like to lose things you thought you couldn't live without. I know what it feels like to sit in the rubble and wonder if anything good could come from it. But I also know this: God never lets suffering have the final word. Favor always writes the last sentence.

So here's what I came to tell you—your double is coming. Not because you earned it. Not because you figured everything out. But because you endured what was meant to destroy you. And now, God is preparing to restore you in ways that make no natural sense.

Favor doesn't forget what you've been through. It adds value to it.

Don't curse this season. Don't shrink back in the silence. The chapter you're in may feel like loss, but

God is already drafting the next one—and it reads: "Double for the damage."

Scripture Focus:

"The Lord restored the fortunes of Job when he prayed for his friends, and the Lord increased all that Job had twofold." — Job 42:10 (NASB 1995)

Reflection Question:

What pain are you holding that God may be asking you to release so favor can flow?

Declaration:

I may have suffered loss, but I'm positioned for restoration. What the enemy meant for destruction, God is turning into double.

CHAPTER 12: CHOSEN WITHOUT CREDENTIALS

E sther had no royal blood. No name that carried weight. No formal training in diplomacy or palace protocol. She was an orphan, raised in exile, a young woman trying to survive in a foreign land. And yet—favor chose her anyway.

"The king loved Esther more than all the women, and she found favor and kindness with him more than all the virgins, so that he set the royal crown on her head and made her queen…"

— Esther 2:17 (NASB 1995)

Let's sit in that for a moment.

Esther didn't have the résumé—but she had the oil. She didn't have the background—but she had the beauty of obedience. She didn't claw her way into the palace—she was positioned there by a plan she couldn't even see.

That's what favor does.

Favor doesn't check your pedigree. It doesn't ask for a LinkedIn profile. It doesn't wait until you have the right letters behind your name. It moves when God says move, and it elevates who God says elevate.

Favor is not a result of qualifications—it's the evidence of God's election.

Esther didn't have to compete—she just had to be ready. She trusted the process. She honored the preparation. She listened to the instructions of Mordecai and Hegai, her advisors. And when the time came, she walked into the presence of the king with confidence—not because of who she was, but because of Who was with her.

That's the secret of favor—it flows through surrender. Esther never forced her way into the crown. She walked into it by grace, through obedience.

And don't miss this: her favor wasn't for decoration —it was for deliverance.

The crown on her head wasn't just about personal

elevation. It was about divine positioning. God placed her in the palace not just to bless her—but to use her. Her favor opened the door for her to rescue an entire nation.

That's how God works. He will bless you in public to use you in private. He'll position you for influence, not for ego, but for impact.

And maybe, like Esther, you feel unqualified. You're questioning your voice, your place, your worth. You see others with more experience, more connections, more visibility. But favor says, "You're still the one."

You may not have the credentials, but you've got the call. You may not have the crown yet, but the oil has already marked you. Favor knows your name—even when the room doesn't.

And when it's time, God will make sure you're seen. Not because of self-promotion, but because of divine timing. You won't have to beg. You won't have to prove. You'll just be chosen.

So stop disqualifying yourself based on where you started. Favor isn't about where you came from—it's about where God is taking you.

Your story—your pain, your struggle, your background—it's not in the way. It's the evidence that when favor shows up, nothing is too broken, too late, or too ordinary to be used.

Scripture Focus:

"The king loved Esther more than all the women, and she found favor and kindness with him more than all the virgins, so that he set the royal crown on her head and made her queen..." — Esther 2:17 (NASB 1995)

Reflection Question:

Where have you been disqualifying yourself that God may be calling you anyway?

Declaration:

I am chosen, not by credentials, but by favor. I may not look the part, but I carry the oil—and God will use me for something greater than I imagined.

CHAPTER 13:
WHEN FAVOR
FINDS YOU
ANYWAY

Some of us have been told our whole lives that we're not the "right kind" of person for certain blessings. You didn't go to the right school. You didn't grow up in the right family. You don't have the platform, the pedigree, or the polish. You're not the type people pick.

Good.

Because favor doesn't pick the expected—it picks the available.

That's the power of Amos's story.

"Then Amos replied to Amaziah, 'I am not a prophet,

nor am I the son of a prophet; for I am a herdsman and a grower of sycamore figs. But the Lord took me from following the flock, and the Lord said to me, 'Go prophesy to My people Israel.'"

— Amos 7:14–15 (NASB 1995)

Amos wasn't raised in ministry. He wasn't from a prophetic bloodline. He wasn't trained in religious circles. He was a farmer—a fig picker and a shepherd. Just a working man doing what he knew to do.

But God took him from the field and gave him a voice that shook a nation.

That's favor.

Favor doesn't look for legacy—it creates one. It doesn't need permission from tradition to move. When God marks you, no résumé can outshine His hand. And when He sends you, no man can un-send you.

Amos didn't apply for the job—he was assigned to it.

This is the part we often miss: Favor doesn't need you to be famous—it needs you to be faithful.

Amos didn't chase a platform. He was following sheep when God called his name. He didn't rehearse a speech. He didn't curate a brand. He just obeyed. And that obedience became the doorway to destiny.

Some of you are waiting to feel "ready" before you step into what God is calling you to. But favor isn't about readiness—it's about response. God doesn't call the qualified. He qualifies the called. And the only thing He needs is your yes.

Let me say it this way: God doesn't need your background—He needs your belief.

If you keep measuring your future by your history, you'll talk yourself out of your assignment. You'll stay in the field picking figs while heaven is calling you to prophesy. You'll let impostor syndrome drown out God's voice.

But favor doesn't check credentials. It checks availability.

God looked past the priests and the prophets and chose Amos. Because sometimes favor skips the stage and finds you in the dirt. In the middle of the ordinary. In the unnoticed places. Not to impress people—but to shift atmospheres.

And here's the truth: If God can use Amos, He can use you.

You may be overlooked by people, but you're not invisible to God. His favor doesn't forget fields. It finds faithfulness.

So stop telling God who you're not. Stop rehearsing your limitations. Start listening for your assignment.

Because favor has a way of finding people who stopped looking for it.

Scripture Focus:

"But the Lord took me from following the flock, and the Lord said to me, 'Go prophesy to My people Israel.'" — Amos 7:15 (NASB 1995)

Reflection Question:

What excuses have you been using to stay in the field when God is calling you to speak?

Declaration:

I am not defined by where I started. I am called, chosen, and favored—right in the middle of the ordinary. If God sends me, I will go.

CHAPTER 14: ACCELERATED BY FAVOR

S ome people rise through the ranks, climbing slowly, step by step. But then there are others —people like Solomon—who seem to leap forward, not because they're striving harder, but because favor fast-tracks what grace has already approved.

Solomon didn't fight like David. He didn't run from caves, dodge spears, or battle giants. His story was different. God gave him something you can't buy, teach, or manipulate: wisdom beyond his years.

"Now God gave Solomon wisdom and very great discernment and breadth of mind, like the sand that is on the seashore. Solomon's wisdom surpassed the wisdom of all the sons of the east and all the wisdom of Egypt."

— 1 Kings 4:29–30 (NASB 1995)

That's not normal. That's not earned. That's favor.

God skipped the slow climb and gave Solomon divine acceleration. It wasn't about hustle—it was about alignment. Because favor doesn't operate on man-made timelines. It moves at the speed of assignment.

While others were gathering experience, Solomon was being graced. And the wisdom God gave him didn't just make him intelligent—it made him influential. Kings and queens traveled just to hear him speak. Solutions flowed from him. Strategy lived in him. Peace surrounded him.

That's what favor does. It puts you ahead of the curve, not to make you boastful, but to make you useful.

Now, I'm not saying your story will look exactly like Solomon's. But I am saying this: when you walk in God's favor, He will put a supernatural wind behind your steps. What should take ten years might take ten months. What you thought you needed credentials for, God may just give you clarity for. What you thought would come through striving, God will release through surrender.

Some of you reading this have been measuring your pace against other people's progress. You've been asking, "Why haven't I arrived yet?" or "How did they get there before me?" But what if I told you: you don't need to chase the timeline—you need to trust the favor.

God knows how to catch you up without you burning out.

Solomon didn't ask for wealth or fame—he asked for wisdom. And God said, "Because you asked for the right thing, I'm giving you what you didn't even ask for." That's favor—overflow that comes from right priorities.

So here's the secret: Seek purpose over position. Character over clout. Wisdom over wealth. And favor will do the rest.

You may feel behind. You may think you've missed your moment. But God doesn't operate on deadlines —He operates on destiny. And favor doesn't play by the rules of time; it redeems time.

Let me make it plain: What others work for, you'll walk in—not because you're better, but because you're favored.

So stop stressing the pace. Stay focused on the presence. Because favor will put you where your feet couldn't go without Him.

Scripture Focus:

"Now God gave Solomon wisdom and very great discernment and breadth of mind…" — 1 Kings 4:29 (NASB 1995)

Reflection Question:

Where have you been striving for things that favor could accomplish through surrender?

Declaration:

I am not behind. I am aligned. God's favor is accelerating my life with wisdom, strategy, and peace. I walk at the speed of purpose.

CHAPTER 15: FOUND IN THE FIELD

Some people are called to the palace. Others are carried there.

Mephibosheth wasn't looking for a throne. He wasn't planning a comeback. He wasn't trying to work his way up or prove himself worthy. He was just surviving in a place called Lo-Debar—a barren land that literally means "no pasture," a dry place with no future.

But then favor came looking for him.

"Then King David sent and brought him from the house of Machir... David said to him, 'Do not fear, for I will surely show kindness to you for the sake of your father Jonathan... and you shall eat at my table regularly.'"

— 2 Samuel 9:5–7 (NASB 1995)

Mephibosheth wasn't just forgotten—he was crippled. Dropped by life. Hidden from the spotlight. Haunted by a past that wasn't even his fault. And yet, none of that disqualified him from the table.

That's favor.

Favor will find you in the most broken, hidden, discarded places—not because of your strength, but because of God's covenant.

David didn't send for Mephibosheth out of sentiment—he did it out of loyalty to a promise he made to Jonathan. And let me tell you something: there are blessings headed your way not because of what you've done, but because of what God already said.

You may feel unqualified. You may feel like time has passed you by. You may think your best years are behind you. But favor says otherwise. Favor doesn't just restore position—it restores identity.

David doesn't just bring Mephibosheth to Jerusalem. He seats him at the king's table—as a son.

Catch that. Not a guest. Not a servant. A son.

That's the power of favor. It takes what life tried to break and calls it belonging. It lifts the overlooked. It heals what was dropped. It rewrites the narrative.

Mephibosheth had every reason to stay hidden.

He was the grandson of Saul, the fallen king. He probably lived with shame, fear, and insecurity. But when the call came from the king, grace overruled guilt. He didn't walk into favor—he was carried into it.

And that's some of us, isn't it?

We've been living in Lo-Debar—settling for less, hiding from purpose, believing we're too broken to be used. But favor isn't intimidated by your condition. God's kindness is stronger than your limp.

You don't have to chase the throne when the King is already calling your name.

There's a seat with your name on it. Not because you earned it. Not because you deserve it. But because God made a promise—to redeem what was broken, to restore what was lost, and to elevate what the world cast aside.

And when you get to that table, don't let the limp define you. The favor covers it. At the table, everyone looks the same. At the table, you belong. At the table, your past has no power—only God's promise does.

Scripture Focus:

"You shall eat at my table regularly." — 2 Samuel 9:7 (NASB 1995)

Reflection Question:

Where have you allowed brokenness or shame to keep you in hiding from what God wants to restore?

Declaration:

I am not forgotten. I am not forsaken. Favor has found me, and there's a seat for me at the King's table. I belong because He called me.

CHAPTER 16: WHEN OUTSIDERS BECOME INSTRUMENTS

God has a way of using the most unlikely people to accomplish the most divine purposes. He doesn't always raise up someone from within the circle. Sometimes, He reaches outside the expected, the acceptable, even the religious, and chooses someone no one saw coming.

That's what makes Cyrus so fascinating.

"This is what the Lord says to Cyrus His anointed,

whom I have taken by the right hand, to subdue nations before him and to undo the weapons belt on the waist of kings..."

— Isaiah 45:1 (NASB 1995)

Cyrus wasn't an Israelite. He wasn't a prophet. He wasn't even a believer in Yahweh. Yet God calls him "His anointed." That's right—anointed. Not because Cyrus understood God's ways, but because God understood how to use Cyrus.

That's favor.

Favor doesn't always flow through familiar vessels. Sometimes it comes through unexpected channels. God will touch the heart of a king who doesn't even know Him to unlock doors on your behalf. He'll use people outside the faith, outside your comfort zone, outside your assumptions—to bless, build, and release you.

Because God's sovereignty isn't limited to church buildings. He's Lord over everything.

This is important: Cyrus didn't ask to be used. He didn't go seeking God's approval. But God put His hand on Cyrus anyway and positioned him to release God's people from captivity. The Israelites had been in Babylonian exile for seventy years, and the one who decreed their freedom wasn't a priest— it was a Persian king.

Sometimes the favor on your life will speak to people

who don't even understand why they're blessing you. It won't make sense to them—but it's divine strategy.

Favor can come from unexpected faces.

That boss who's not saved but just gave you a promotion? Favor.

That investor who doesn't share your values but opened a door for your vision? Favor.

That stranger who extended generosity at the exact moment you needed it most? Favor.

God is not bound by what makes sense. He's bound by His Word.

And when He decides to move, He doesn't need to consult your list of qualifications or check anyone's résumé. He just does it.

Cyrus was raised up for one reason: to fulfill God's purpose. He was given access, authority, and anointing—not because of merit, but because of mission.

And that's how God will work in your life, too.

Don't be surprised if God uses someone outside your circle to open a door you've been praying about. Don't reject the vessel just because it doesn't look like what you expected. Favor isn't about how it arrives—it's about what it accomplishes.

And here's the best part: when God uses outsiders,

He reminds the insiders that He is God all by Himself.

He doesn't need your perfect performance. He just needs your positioning.

So stop trying to predict how God will move. He's not interested in fitting your formula. He's interested in fulfilling His plan. And sometimes, that plan includes kings named Cyrus.

Scripture Focus:

"This is what the Lord says to Cyrus His anointed..." — Isaiah 45:1 (NASB 1995)

Reflection Question:

Are you open to God using unexpected people and pathways to release favor in your life?

Declaration:

I won't limit how God can bless me. Favor isn't always familiar—it's often strategic. Even unlikely vessels can carry supernatural breakthroughs.

CHAPTER 17:
POSITIONED FOR
INFLUENCE

S ome people fight to be seen. Others are positioned to be noticed—not because they demanded the spotlight, but because they carried something excellence couldn't ignore.

That was Daniel.

Exiled from his homeland. Stripped of his heritage. Given a new name in a foreign kingdom. And yet, favor didn't fade. It followed. Not only did Daniel survive Babylon—he rose in it.

"Then this Daniel began distinguishing himself among the commissioners and satraps because he possessed an extraordinary spirit, and the king intended to appoint him over the entire kingdom."

— Daniel 6:3 (NASB 1995)

He wasn't a politician. He wasn't a Babylonian. He wasn't trying to climb the ladder. Daniel simply carried an "extraordinary spirit." That's Bible code for: favor was on him.

You need to hear this—you don't have to manipulate your way into rooms God has already reserved for you. Daniel didn't scheme. He didn't cut corners. He just remained faithful, excellent, consistent. And in a culture that constantly shifted, that kind of integrity stood out.

That's what favor does.

Favor elevates character over charisma. It highlights those who show up when others shrink back. It draws attention not to arrogance—but to anointing.

Notice what Scripture says: the king intended to place him over the whole kingdom. That's influence. But not influence Daniel chased—influence God arranged.

We often think favor is about being the loudest voice in the room. But Daniel teaches us: favor flows through quiet faithfulness. It rises through prayer, through discipline, through devotion when no one is watching.

And watch this—Daniel didn't earn favor by being perfect. He earned it by being set apart. He prayed when it was illegal. He honored God when it wasn't popular. He stayed steady when the culture bowed.

And because of that, favor lifted him.

Here's what that means for you: You don't need to be loud to be lifted. You don't need to announce yourself when God has already placed His hand on you. Just be faithful with what you've been given, and watch God open doors that no résumé ever could.

And don't be surprised if your influence grows in places that feel foreign. Daniel was in Babylon —not Jerusalem. His favor thrived in a secular environment. Because God doesn't need the conditions to be perfect to show His glory.

Your location doesn't limit your elevation.

The same Spirit that set Daniel apart is still setting people apart today. Not the most popular. Not the most polished. But the most faithful.

If you stay consistent, if you walk in character, if you honor God behind the scenes—favor will find you, and influence will follow.

Don't chase position—chase presence. And favor will position you exactly where you're called to be.

Scripture Focus:

"Then this Daniel began distinguishing himself... because he possessed an extraordinary spirit." —

Daniel 6:3 (NASB 1995)

Reflection Question:

Are you cultivating what makes you distinct, or are you trying to blend in where favor has called you to stand out?

Declaration:

I don't have to fight for favor. I will walk in faithfulness, and God will position me for influence in every season and space.

CHAPTER 18: FAVOR IN THE FIRE

There are seasons when being faithful will land you in the fire instead of the spotlight. Seasons where obedience gets you thrown down instead of lifted up. When standing for truth doesn't earn you applause—it earns you a pit.

That's what happened to Jeremiah.

He wasn't preaching popularity. He wasn't chasing platforms. He was declaring the Word of the Lord in a time when people didn't want to hear it. And for that, he was lowered into a cistern—an empty well, filled with mud.

"So they pulled Jeremiah up with ropes and lifted him out of the cistern..."

— Jeremiah 38:13 (NASB 1995)

Favor doesn't always keep you out of the pit. Sometimes it shows up in the pit with ropes.

Jeremiah was doing exactly what God told him to do, and yet he found himself sinking in mud, alone, discarded, silenced. But even in that dark place, favor hadn't forgotten him.

Because favor doesn't disappear in the struggle. It just works behind the scenes.

God moved on the heart of an unlikely advocate —Ebed-melech, an Ethiopian eunuch in the king's court—who spoke up and rescued Jeremiah. No announcement. No angels. Just one man, some old rags, and a rope. That's favor: God moving through ordinary means to produce extraordinary outcomes.

And hear me clearly—you might be in a muddy, forgotten place right now, but you are not forsaken. Favor hasn't skipped you. It's preparing the rope.

Some of the greatest works of favor happen when we can't see them. When you feel buried, dismissed, written off. But favor is still flowing. It's speaking your name in rooms you haven't entered yet. It's stirring hearts to come find you. It's aligning the moment where the rope will drop, and the lifting will begin.

Here's what makes this story powerful: Jeremiah

didn't have to climb out. He was pulled out. That's grace. That's God saying, "This pit won't be your grave. It'll be your platform."

Sometimes we assume favor means everything will go smoothly. But ask Jeremiah—sometimes favor will let you be thrown down so God can show off when He brings you back up.

And maybe that's your story. Maybe you've been cast aside, criticized, isolated for standing in truth. Don't quit. Don't silence your voice. God's favor isn't finished just because you feel stuck.

God knows how to send the right person with the right rope at the right time. It may not be flashy. It may not be fast. But it will be faithful.

So hold on in the mud. Lift your eyes. Because favor doesn't forget cisterns—it redeems them.

Scripture Focus:

"So they pulled Jeremiah up with ropes and lifted him out of the cistern..." — Jeremiah 38:13 (NASB 1995)

Reflection Question:

Where in your life do you feel stuck that God may be preparing to pull you out of?

Declaration:

Even when I feel forgotten, I am favored. God is sending the rope. What was meant to sink me will become the place where He lifts me.

CHAPTER 19: PROVISION IN UNLIKELY PLACES

Sometimes the need shows up before the resource. The bill hits before the check. The pressure mounts before the plan is clear. And in those moments, it's tempting to panic, to grasp, to hustle.

But favor doesn't panic—it provides.

Jesus and Peter were confronted about the temple tax. A small detail, but it carried weight. These weren't just religious dues; they were cultural expectations. And Peter, like most of us, probably felt the tension: "We don't have it—what now?"

But Jesus wasn't worried. He wasn't scrambling for coins. He gave Peter an unusual instruction:

"Go to the sea and throw in a hook, and take the first fish that comes up; and when you open its mouth, you will find a shekel. Take that and give it to them for you and Me."

— Matthew 17:27 (NASB 1995)

A coin... in a fish's mouth.

Let that settle in.

Jesus didn't tell Peter to borrow it. He didn't multiply coins like He did with loaves and fish. He sent him to the water. To do something that didn't make financial sense but made faith sense.

That's what favor does.

Favor doesn't always come from expected places. Sometimes it shows up in obedience to an odd instruction. Sometimes provision is hidden inside the familiar—Peter was a fisherman, after all. Jesus used what Peter already knew, but gave it a supernatural twist.

Provision was waiting in Peter's profession.

God didn't drop the coin from the sky. He sent Peter back to what he was already gifted in. But this time, favor was flowing through it.

Some of you are praying for a financial miracle, a breakthrough, a provision moment—and God is pointing you right back to what you already do. Your gift. Your grind. Your "ordinary." Because favor often hides in the places we overlook.

And don't miss this: Jesus said, "Take the first fish." That means Peter didn't have to catch 10 or wait all day. The provision was in the first step of obedience.

The favor you're looking for might be tied to your first yes.

It wasn't about the fish—it was about Peter trusting the Word. God wanted to show him (and us) that He can provide in any way, at any time, through any method.

God doesn't run out of ways to meet your need.

Don't limit Him to a paycheck, a person, or a particular path. Favor isn't limited by what's in your hand—it's powered by what's in His mouth.

When Jesus speaks a Word, creation responds. Even fish swim with provision on their lips when favor is at work.

So what is God telling you to cast again? Where is He pointing that doesn't make sense but feels full of peace? That's where the favor is. Don't ignore it just because it doesn't look "logical."

Favor flows through obedience—especially when the instruction feels unusual.

The coin is already in the water. All God needs is your willingness to cast the line.

Scripture Focus:

"Take the first fish... and when you open its mouth, you will find a shekel." — Matthew 17:27 (NASB 1995)

Reflection Question:

What area of your life is God pointing to for unexpected provision?

Declaration:

I won't fear the lack—I will trust the instruction. God's favor brings provision from unexpected places, and I will find it in obedience.

CHAPTER 20: FAVOR TURNS A "NO" INTO A NEW ROUTE

You prayed. You planned. You positioned yourself. And still, the door slammed shut. Not gently—loud, jarring, and final. You thought you heard God. You thought this was the right move. But now you're staring at a closed opportunity, wondering where you missed it.

Paul knew that feeling.

In Acts 16, Paul and his team were on a mission. They weren't chasing comfort—they were chasing purpose. But as they tried to enter Asia, the Holy Spirit blocked them. Then they tried Bithynia. Another no. No explanation. No reason. Just...

blocked.

"They passed through the Phrygian and Galatian region, having been forbidden by the Holy Spirit to speak the word in Asia... and the Spirit of Jesus did not allow them."

— Acts 16:6–7 (NASB 1995)

That's not how we expect favor to operate, is it?

We think favor means green lights. Wide doors. Open paths. But sometimes, favor shows up as a "no"—not because you're off course, but because God is about to reroute you into something greater.

Let me tell you what I've learned: Favor isn't always permission. Sometimes, it's prevention.

God wasn't punishing Paul—He was positioning him. Because right after the closed doors, Paul had a vision. A man from Macedonia crying out, "Come help us." And just like that, favor revealed the real assignment.

Macedonia wasn't Plan B. It was heaven's Plan A.

Favor doesn't just open the right doors. It closes the wrong ones.

We cry over blocked paths, not realizing they saved us time, energy, and unnecessary detours. Sometimes God's "no" is the most profound form of favor, because it keeps you from spending years in something He never endorsed.

And here's the part we often miss—Paul only got the "yes" after he surrendered to the "no." He didn't pitch a tent in frustration. He didn't force his way in. He kept moving.

Some of us are stuck, not because God hasn't spoken, but because we're still grieving the door He already closed. But favor doesn't linger in locked places. It leads.

God is not in the business of wasting purpose. If a door is shut, it means what's behind it isn't for you —or isn't ready for you. Either way, favor knows the difference.

And when you walk in favor, your direction doesn't come from what feels open—it comes from Who is leading.

Paul's redirection led him to Philippi—where a woman named Lydia would be the first convert, a church would be born, and a letter would one day be written that's still changing lives.

One closed door shifted the trajectory of the Gospel.

So let me ask you: What are you still calling rejection that might actually be redirection?

God sees the map. You see the moment. And favor is not lost—it's leading. Even if the route changes, the promise doesn't.

Scripture Focus:

"They were forbidden by the Holy Spirit to speak the word in Asia… and the Spirit of Jesus did not allow them." — Acts 16:6–7 (NASB 1995)

Reflection Question:

What closed door are you still grieving that favor may have used to redirect you?

Declaration:

I trust the detour. Favor doesn't just open doors—it closes them for my protection. I will follow where God leads, even when the route changes.

CHAPTER 21: FAVOR FINDS YOU IN THE FIELD

We think favor finds us on the stage. In the spotlight. After the applause. But some of God's most powerful promotions happen in the field—in the quiet, mundane places where nobody's watching and nothing seems to be changing.

That's where Elisha was when everything shifted.

"So he departed from there and found Elisha the son of Shaphat, while he was plowing with twelve pairs of oxen before him... and Elijah passed over to him and threw his mantle on him."

— 1 Kings 19:19 (NASB 1995)

Elisha wasn't fasting on a mountain. He wasn't

leading a revival. He was plowing. Sweaty. Ordinary. Faithful. Day after day in the dirt. But that's where favor found him—in the middle of consistency.

Favor doesn't need a stage. It looks for stewardship.

Elijah didn't call out for résumés. He didn't post an opportunity. He walked by, saw Elisha working, and dropped the mantle.

And just like that, everything changed.

Let this sink in: Elisha didn't chase the mantle—the mantle found him. Why? Because God promotes those who are already plowing.

We live in a culture that says, "Go viral, get noticed, build your brand." But God's strategy is different: "Be faithful where I placed you, and I'll find you when it's time."

Some of the most anointed people are still in the field. Still showing up. Still unseen. Still steady. And God is not overlooking you—He's watching your plow.

Favor doesn't look for flashy. It looks for faithful.

And when the time comes, the mantle won't miss you.

Here's what's powerful: Elisha left everything when the call came. He didn't hesitate. He didn't say, "Let me finish this row." He burned the plow. Killed the oxen. Fed the people. Then followed Elijah.

That's what favor demands—a full yes.

When God calls you out of the field, you don't bring the plow with you. You let go of the old to embrace the next.

And some of you... you're on the verge of that moment.

You've been faithful. You've been working. You've been wondering, "God, does this matter?" And the answer is: yes.

The plow prepared you for the platform. The dirt shaped your depth. The repetition built your resilience. And now, favor is about to find you—in the field, in the ordinary, on a Tuesday that feels like any other.

But this time, the prophet's coming.

The call is coming.

And when it does, everything will shift—not because you chased it, but because you were ready for it.

Scripture Focus:

"Elijah passed over to him and threw his mantle on him." — 1 Kings 19:19 (NASB 1995)

Reflection Question:

Where have you been faithful in private that God may be preparing to honor in public?

Declaration:

I don't need to chase favor—I just need to keep plowing. God sees my field, and when the time is right, He will call me forward.

CHAPTER 22: WHEN FAVOR REWRITES YOUR REPUTATION

Some people know your past.

God knows your future.

And when favor steps in, it doesn't ask for permission to transform your story—it just does. That's what happened with Mary Magdalene. She wasn't known for her resume. She was known for her reputation. And it wasn't a good one.

"Soon afterward, Jesus began going around... also some women who had been healed of evil spirits and sicknesses: Mary who was called Magdalene, from whom seven demons had gone out..."

— Luke 8:1–2 (NASB 1995)

That's how Scripture first introduces her. Mary—delivered. Mary—set free. Mary—marked by grace.

She didn't grow up in the temple. She wasn't trained like the disciples. She was a woman with a history. A woman with scars. A woman who'd been through hell—but favor met her anyway.

And after that moment? Everything changed.

Mary didn't just become a follower—she became a funder. She supported Jesus' ministry with her resources. She was one of the few who stayed at the cross when others ran. And she was the first witness of the resurrection.

That's not a coincidence. That's favor.

Favor doesn't ignore your past—it overrides it.

It doesn't pretend your mistakes didn't happen. It just refuses to let them define who you become.

Mary Magdalene's life is proof that you don't have to be the cleanest, calmest, or most "churchy" person to be used by God. You just have to be willing.

Jesus didn't disqualify her because of what she'd battled—He called her because of what she was becoming.

Let that encourage you: Your reputation might make people uncomfortable, but it doesn't intimidate heaven. God isn't limited by what they say about you. He's moved by what He's placed in you.

Mary's favor didn't just restore her dignity—it redefined her destiny. From outcast to eyewitness. From marked by demons to marked by history.

Some of you have been carrying labels that favor is ready to break. You've been held hostage by who you used to be, what you used to do, or what people still whisper when your name comes up.

But favor says, "Watch what I do with the one they counted out."

Mary Magdalene became a pillar in Jesus' ministry. Not because she came from status—but because she came with surrender.

Don't let your past talk you out of your future.

When Jesus sets you free, you're free indeed—and favored, too.

The same woman who had seven demons is now forever remembered as the first one to see the resurrected Savior. That's not luck. That's the kind of favor that rewrites legacies.

And guess what? If God did it for her, He can do it for you.

Scripture Focus:

"Mary who was called Magdalene, from whom seven demons had gone out." — Luke 8:2 (NASB 1995)

Reflection Question:

What label from your past is God ready to replace with a new identity?

Declaration:

My past will not disqualify me. Favor is rewriting my story. I am no longer who I was—God is making me into who I'm meant to be.

CHAPTER 23: FAVOR FOLLOWS FORGIVENESS

L et's talk about what favor looks like after the betrayal. After the heartbreak. After the people closest to you did the most damage. Because real favor isn't just about what God gives you—it's about what doesn't break you.

And no one understood that better than Joseph.

"Then Joseph said to his brothers, 'Please come closer to me'... 'I am your brother Joseph, whom you sold to Egypt. Now do not be grieved... because God sent me ahead of you to preserve life.'"

— Genesis 45:4–5 (NASB 1995)

That's not bitterness speaking. That's not sarcasm. That's clarity. That's favor matured by fire.

Joseph had every right to flex. Every reason to make them sweat. These were the same brothers who stripped him of his coat, threw him in a pit, and sold him like property. And yet—when he had the upper hand, he opened his heart instead.

Why?

Because favor doesn't seek revenge. Favor remembers the pit but refuses to live in it.

Joseph understood something most of us spend years trying to grasp: the assignment was bigger than the offense. What they meant for evil, God used for good. What tried to break him, built him. What looked like betrayal became the bridge to destiny.

And here's the kicker: Joseph's favor didn't fully unlock until he forgave.

He had already risen in Egypt. He was already second-in-command. But it wasn't until he released what happened that he realized why it had to happen. Some of us are favored, but still bound. Gifted, but still gripped by what they did.

Let me say this plainly: You can't walk in the fullness of favor while dragging the chains of unforgiveness. Not because God's withholding—because you're still holding on.

Forgiveness is not saying it didn't hurt. It's saying, "It can't hold me hostage anymore."

It's refusing to let your betrayers become your

blueprint. It's trusting that God can turn the worst chapter into the very platform for your purpose.

Joseph didn't just survive the pit, the prison, or the palace. He transcended them. And when his brothers showed up hungry, broken, and guilty—he saw them not as enemies, but as instruments.

That's the mark of favor.

It transforms how you see the people who tried to destroy you. It takes you from vengeance to vision. From "Why me?" to "God sent me."

Maybe that's where you are.

Maybe God has raised you up.

Maybe you're standing in a better place now—but still battling the pain of the people who hurt you on the way there.

Let Joseph remind you: you're not in that position just to shine. You're there to save. And sometimes, the people who need saving are the very ones who wounded you.

Forgive them—not for them, but for you. Because your future is too weighty to carry their offense any longer.

Favor is calling. And it sounds a lot like freedom.

Scripture Focus:

"God sent me ahead of you to preserve life." — Genesis 45:5 (NASB 1995)

Reflection Question:

What unresolved hurt is holding space in your heart that forgiveness could finally clear out?

Declaration:

I release what they did. I embrace what God's doing. Favor follows forgiveness, and I won't miss my future carrying old pain.

CHAPTER 24: WHEN FAVOR COVERS THE FALL

F ailure has a way of echoing. It doesn't just knock you down—it names you. And if you're not careful, you'll start answering to labels that grace never assigned: Unworthy. Disqualified. Disgrace.

That's exactly where Peter found himself.

He wasn't just a disciple. He was the disciple—the loud one, the bold one, the walk-on-water one. He swore he'd never leave Jesus. But when pressure hit, when accusations flew, Peter folded.

Three times he denied the One he said he'd die for. And after the rooster crowed, shame didn't whisper —it shouted.

But favor had the final word.

"Jesus said to him, 'Simon, son of John, do you love Me?... Feed My sheep.'"

— John 21:15–17 (NASB 1995)

Jesus didn't show up to condemn Peter. He came to restore him.

That's what favor does.

It doesn't ignore your fall. It redeems it. Jesus didn't sweep the betrayal under the rug. He brought it into the light—not to shame Peter, but to recommission him.

Three denials.

Three questions.

Three declarations of love.

And each one was a key turning back the lock Peter thought was sealed forever.

Favor doesn't just forgive your failure—it folds it into your future.

Jesus didn't remove Peter from the team. He put him in charge. "Feed My sheep," He said. In other words, "Your fall didn't cancel your call."

Let that sink in. Peter's worst moment became the backdrop for his greatest assignment. He went from denying Christ to declaring Him boldly in front of thousands. From the shadows to the stage. From brokenness to boldness.

That's not talent. That's not hustle.

That's favor.

Maybe you've disqualified yourself because of something you did—or failed to do. Maybe you've let shame steal your seat at the table. But here's the truth: God never stopped calling your name.

Your failure doesn't threaten His faithfulness.

Your fall doesn't cancel His favor.

You're still in the story. And grace has already rewritten your next chapter.

Jesus didn't ask Peter, "Why did you fail?"

He asked, "Do you love Me?"

Because love is the only qualification favor requires.

And if you can answer that—if you can still say yes even through the tears, the regret, the limp—then you're right where you need to be. Favor has found you. Not to put you back where you were, but to lift you into who you're becoming.

The rooster may have crowed. But the Redeemer has spoken louder.

Scripture Focus:

"Jesus said to him... 'Feed My sheep.'" – John 21:17

(NASB 1995)

Reflection Question:

What failure have you allowed to define you that Jesus already forgave?

Declaration:

My failure is not final. Jesus has restored me, and favor is still flowing. I will feed the sheep. I will finish strong.

CHAPTER 25: FROM BARREN TO BLESSED

Some breakthroughs don't come quickly. Some favor doesn't shout—it waits. And in that waiting, in that seemingly barren season, you start to wonder: Did God forget me?

That was Hannah's question.

She loved God. She worshiped faithfully. But month after month, year after year—no child. No answer. No shift. Meanwhile, her rival Peninnah flaunted what Hannah was still praying for. Taunted her. Mocked her. Reminded her of what she lacked.

And yet, Hannah didn't lash out. She didn't give up. She went into the temple and poured her soul out to God.

"For this boy I prayed, and.the Lord has granted me my request which I asked of Him."

— 1 Samuel 1:27 (NASB 1995)

Hannah teaches us that favor isn't always fast. It's formed in persistence. In private prayers that sound like groans. In worship that presses past disappointment. In tears that nobody else understands—but heaven hears.

Favor doesn't just show up at the birth—it begins in the barrenness.

Hannah didn't stop praying just because the answer hadn't come. She sowed faith in famine. She kept believing when her womb said otherwise. And that kind of posture pulls on heaven.

When she finally held Samuel, her miracle child, she didn't hoard the blessing—she returned it. Gave him back to God. Because Hannah understood: favor isn't about getting more—it's about stewarding what God gives with surrender.

And that's the difference between favor and fortune. Favor doesn't feed ego. It fuels impact.

Samuel didn't just become a child. He became a prophet. A priest. A king-maker. He changed nations because his mother changed her posture in the waiting room.

Maybe that's where you are.

Still waiting. Still believing. Still battling the silence. Can I tell you something?

Your prayers are pregnant.

Your tears are not wasted.

And the God who heard Hannah hasn't gone deaf to you.

Don't stop showing up. Don't stop pouring out. The womb may be empty now, but favor is forming something in secret. And when the time is right, the blessing will not be small. It will carry purpose. It will carry weight.

And like Hannah, you'll be able to say: "For this I prayed. And the Lord granted it."

Not because of your perfection. But because of your persistence.

Favor isn't afraid of long seasons. It lives in surrendered ones.

Scripture Focus:

"For this boy I prayed, and the Lord has granted me my request which I asked of Him." — 1 Samuel 1:27 (NASB 1995)

Reflection Question:

What have you stopped praying for that God may still be preparing?

Declaration:

My delay is not my denial. I will keep praying, keep pressing, and keep trusting. Favor is forming what my eyes haven't seen yet—but my faith still believes.

CHAPTER 26: POSITIONED AT THE RIGHT GATE

Sometimes favor doesn't look like a promotion —it looks like a pattern. Day after day. Same problem. Same place. Same pain.

That's where the man at the Beautiful Gate was.

Laid at the entrance.

Carried, but never changed.

Close to breakthrough, but never quite in.

"And a man who had been unable to walk from birth was being carried… whom they used to put daily at the gate of the temple which is called Beautiful, so that he could beg for charitable gifts…"

— Acts 3:2 (NASB 1995)

Imagine the frustration. Living life inches away from the presence of God, yet never entering in. Watching others walk in whole while you sit stuck, waiting on help that only keeps you coping—not healing.

But then favor passed by.

Peter and John didn't just give him money. They gave him what money couldn't buy.

"In the name of Jesus Christ the Nazarene—walk!"

And the Bible says:

"Immediately his feet and ankles were strengthened... and he entered the temple with them, walking and leaping and praising God." — Acts 3:6–8 (NASB 1995)

That's what favor does.

It finds you at the gate.

It interrupts the cycle.

It gives you strength to stand in places where you've only ever sat.

This man was in the right place, even though he was in the wrong condition.

Sometimes, favor is about where you are before it's about what you receive.

He could've given up. Could've stopped showing up. But even broken, even overlooked, even stuck—he stayed close to the temple. And favor found him because he stayed planted.

Let me tell you something powerful:

Just because your situation hasn't shifted yet doesn't mean God has forgotten you.

You may feel like you've been laying in the same place too long, but your positioning matters. Proximity to the presence positions you for a miracle.

And here's the part we often miss: once healed, the man didn't just walk—he leaped. He didn't limp into his future. He ran into it. Favor didn't just restore what was lost—it gave him momentum to move forward.

That's what God is about to do for someone reading this.

He's not just going to help you stand. He's going to help you soar.

Favor won't just fix what's broken—it will release what's been waiting inside you.

The man at the gate was always more than a beggar. But it took one moment of favor to activate the strength in his legs—and the calling on his life.

So keep showing up. Keep sitting at the gate.

Because when favor walks by, everything changes.

Scripture Focus:

"Immediately his feet and ankles were strengthened." — Acts 3:7 (NASB 1995)

Reflection Question:

Where have you been consistent in a hard place that God may be about to move supernaturally in?

Declaration:

I may feel stuck, but I'm positioned for favor. God is strengthening what's been weak and activating what's been waiting. I won't just walk—I'll leap into what's next.

CHAPTER 27:
GRACE IN
THE GAP

There's a gap between the promise and the performance. A delay between what God said and when it shows up. And in that gap—doubt grows loud. Logic fights faith. Time tests trust.

But favor doesn't fold under the wait.

Favor believes anyway.

That was Abraham's posture.

"Yet, with respect to the promise of God, he did not waver in unbelief but grew strong in faith, giving glory to God, and being fully assured that what God had promised, He was able also to perform."

— Romans 4:20–21 (NASB 1995)

Let's not water this down. Abraham wasn't believing for a parking space. He was believing for a nation —through a barren womb and a body "as good as dead." The numbers didn't add up. The timing didn't make sense. And yet... favor made him firm.

He didn't grow weary—he grew strong.

Not because everything was clear, but because his faith was rooted in the character of the One who made the promise.

Here's the secret: Faith doesn't rely on evidence. It rests on trust.

And trust is the foundation of favor.

Abraham understood something we need to reclaim: God doesn't need ideal conditions to release a supernatural outcome. The promise wasn't based on Sarah's age or his performance—it was based on God's ability.

And that's where we struggle. We try to bring God's Word down to the level of our understanding. We try to calculate favor like it's a formula. But favor is faith in motion. And faith doesn't ask, "How?"—it declares, "He will."

Maybe you're in the gap right now. You've received the word, but haven't seen the results. The delay is stretching you. The silence is unsettling. The wait feels like a weight.

But listen—don't waver.

Don't trade your promise for a plan B.

Don't downgrade your faith just to feel more in control.

Abraham didn't just wait—he worshiped while waiting. He "gave glory to God," not after Isaac was born, but before.

That's favor. It praises on credit.

It thanks God for what's coming, even while standing in what hasn't arrived.

The enemy wants you to think the delay is a denial. That the gap means you missed it. But God says: "I'm still able. I'm still faithful. And I'm still coming through."

The promise still holds. And favor is holding you.

So stay planted. Stay persuaded.

And when you feel weak, remind yourself:

The promise isn't fragile—you're favored.

Scripture Focus:

"…being fully assured that what God had promised, He was able also to perform." — Romans 4:21 (NASB 1995)

Reflection Question:

What promise are you tempted to give up on that God is still planning to fulfill?

Declaration:

I will not waver in the wait. What God promised, He will perform. I'm favored in the gap—and grace is carrying me through it.

CHAPTER 28: FAVOR THAT FINDS THE FORGOTTEN

Sometimes favor doesn't come when you're at the top. It finds you while you're still in the shadows—forgotten, overlooked, counted out.

That's how it was for David.

He wasn't born into royalty. He didn't come from prestige. He was a shepherd, tucked away in the hills, watching sheep while his brothers stood tall in front of Samuel. He was so far off the radar, his own father didn't think to call him when the prophet came looking for a king.

But God did.

"I took you from the pasture, from following the sheep, to be leader over My people Israel. And I have been with you wherever you have gone..."

— 2 Samuel 7:8–9 (NASB 1995)

God reminds David: "I found you when no one else was looking. I lifted you when no one else believed in you. And I've been with you every step since."

That's favor.

Not the kind you earn. Not the kind you chase. The kind that interrupts your life with the unexpected. The kind that pulls you from the background to the front lines. The kind that doesn't need permission from people who overlooked you to elevate you anyway.

Favor doesn't wait for a spotlight. It shines in secret first.

David wasn't trying to be king. He was just being faithful in the pasture. And that's exactly what qualified him. Because while the world celebrates platform, heaven honors preparation.

God said, "I took you from following sheep." Not leading armies. Not writing psalms. Following sheep. In other words: "You knew how to follow before I called you to lead."

That's a word right there.

Some of us are frustrated in the pasture, thinking

we're forgotten. But the pasture is where God proves your posture. It's where He sees if you'll obey in obscurity before He promotes you in visibility.

And let's not miss this: God doesn't just find David —He walks with him. "I have been with you wherever you have gone." That's favor, too. Not just the call, but the companionship. The covering. The covenant.

Favor stays when others walk away. It goes with you into every room, every battle, every high and low.

Maybe you feel invisible right now. You've been working, serving, showing up—and no one sees it. Let this chapter remind you: God sees the pasture. He promotes from the shadows. He elevates the faithful.

And when He calls your name, nothing and no one can block it. Not your background. Not your birth order. Not your experience. Just favor.

God took David from forgotten to favored—and He can do the same for you.

Scripture Focus:

"I took you from the pasture, from following the sheep, to be leader over My people Israel." — 2 Samuel 7:8 (NASB 1995)

Reflection Question:

Where in your life have you mistaken obscurity for being overlooked?

Declaration:

Even in the pasture, I'm favored. God sees me, God is with me, and when the time is right, He will raise me.

CHAPTER 29: FAVOR IN THE FIGHT

S ometimes favor doesn't look like a shield—
It looks like a strategy.

Because while we often pray for God to remove the battle, favor teaches us that sometimes, He doesn't take the fight away—He just steps into it with us.

That's what happened in 2 Chronicles 20.

Jehoshaphat and the people of Judah were surrounded. Outnumbered. Outmatched. Three enemy armies had joined forces against them. They didn't have the manpower, the weapons, or the time to prepare.

But what they did have— was favor.

And here's what God said to them:

"You need not fight in this battle; take your position, stand and watch the salvation of the Lord in your behalf, Judah and Jerusalem."

— 2 Chronicles 20:17 (NASB 1995)

That's a word.

Take your position.

Stand still.

Watch God work.

See, favor doesn't mean you'll never face a fight. It means you'll never have to face it alone.

And in this case, they weren't even asked to throw a punch—just to take a position of praise.

Because the real power wasn't in their weapons. It was in their worship.

Jehoshaphat sent the singers out ahead of the soldiers.

Who does that?

Only people who know they're not fighting for victory—they're standing in favor and fighting from victory.

Sometimes, the most powerful thing you can do in a battle is lift your voice.

Not in fear. In faith.

Not in panic. In praise.

While the worship rose, confusion hit the enemy's camp. The armies that came to destroy Judah turned on each other.

And when Judah showed up the next day, all they had to do was collect the spoils.

That's favor.

It not only secures your survival—it rewards your obedience.

Here's what's wild: the battle lasted a moment, but the blessing lasted days. Scripture says it took three days just to gather all the wealth left behind.

So yes, the fight looked terrifying.

But the favor was greater.

Some of you are facing battles right now that seem impossible. A diagnosis. A legal situation. A financial crisis. A spiritual war in your home.

And the enemy is whispering, "You're not going to make it."

But God is declaring:

"This isn't your battle—it's Mine. Take your position. Lift your hands. Open your mouth. Favor is about to fight for you."

You may not see a way, but Heaven has already written the outcome.

So stand firm.

Sing loud.

And when the dust settles, you won't just survive—you'll be carrying blessings you didn't even ask for.

Scripture Focus:

"You need not fight in this battle; take your position, stand and watch the salvation of the Lord..." — 2 Chronicles 20:17 (NASB 1995)

Reflection Question:

Where do you need to shift from fighting in your strength to standing in God's favor?

Declaration:

This battle isn't mine—it belongs to the Lord. I take my position, I lift my praise, and I receive the victory by faith.

CHAPTER 30: WHEN FAVOR FINDS YOUR FAITHFULNESS

She wasn't royalty.

She wasn't a prophetess.

She wasn't a social media sensation or temple influencer.

Mary was just a teenager in Nazareth—an overlooked town with no reputation for greatness. She wasn't trying to be famous. She was simply faithful.

And then, favor knocked on her door.

"And coming in, the angel said to her, 'Greetings,

favored one! The Lord is with you.' … The angel said to her, 'Do not be afraid, Mary, for you have found favor with God.'"

— Luke 1:28, 30 (NASB 1995)

Let that settle in.

You have found favor with God.

Not because she came from wealth.

Not because she earned it.

Not because she pushed her way to the front.

Mary found favor because she was faithful with who she already was.

She didn't perform for heaven. She simply lived in quiet obedience—and God saw it. He chose her to carry the promise, not because she was the most powerful, but because she was the most willing.

Favor flows through surrender, not spotlight.

And hear this—Mary didn't feel qualified. She was troubled. Confused. She asked, "How can this be?" Like many of us, she looked at her limitations before trusting God's invitation.

But favor wasn't intimidated by her questions. It wasn't canceled by her inexperience. In fact, favor thrives in humility.

Some of us think favor will find us once we finally "arrive." Once we've healed. Once we've achieved.

Once we've built the platform.

But Mary's story proves something powerful:

God doesn't choose you because you're ready. He chooses you because you're available.

Favor doesn't wait until you've got it all figured out. It shows up in the ordinary, in the places where your only qualification is yes.

And here's the part that blesses me: favor didn't just bless Mary—it cost her, too.

It changed her plans.

Stretched her faith.

Risked her reputation.

But still, she said, "Be it unto me according to Your word."

Because favor isn't always comfortable.

It's weighty.

But it always carries purpose.

Maybe God is calling you to carry something bigger than your current capacity.

Maybe He's inviting you into a season that doesn't make sense but will make history.

Say yes.

Even if you're nervous.

Even if you're unsure.

Because favor finds the faithful, not the flawless.

Mary became the mother of Jesus—not because she campaigned for it, but because she surrendered to it.

And if He used her, He can use you.

Scripture Focus:

"Do not be afraid, Mary, for you have found favor with God." — Luke 1:30 (NASB 1995)

Reflection Question:

What assignment might God be inviting you into that requires a fresh "yes"?

Declaration:

I may not feel qualified, but I am favored. My faithfulness has found heaven's attention, and I say yes to what God is calling me to carry.

CHAPTER 31: SURROUNDED BY FAVOR

There's a kind of favor that doesn't just visit —it stays. A covering. A shield. A divine force field around your life that you didn't earn, can't explain, and absolutely cannot live without.

David called it out with boldness:

"For You bless the righteous person, Lord, You surround him with favor as with a shield."

— Psalm 5:12 (NASB 1995)

This isn't a temporary favor. This isn't a "one good thing happened to me today" kind of favor. This is a surrounding. Favor that wraps around your weakness. Favor that stands between you and the enemy. Favor that doesn't leave when circumstances shift.

You don't have to chase what God has already encircled you with.

It's not based on your perfection. It's rooted in His promise.

David wasn't perfect—far from it. But he was righteous, not because he never failed, but because he kept coming back to God. Favor surrounds the ones who remain under His rule.

Think about that word: shield.

A shield isn't passive. It protects. It absorbs what was meant to take you out. It blocks what was designed to break you. That's what favor does. Some of the attacks you never saw weren't because the enemy didn't try—it's because favor intercepted it first.

And here's what makes this so beautiful: the shield doesn't only protect—it advances.

You don't just survive—you move forward with favor.

You show up to the interview? Favor is already in the room.

You step into that courtroom? Favor is seated beside you.

You walk into a situation that looks impossible? Favor has already spoken your name before you arrive.

You are surrounded.

Not just by problems.

Not just by people.

But by promise.

God didn't just save you—He secured you.

And in case you forgot, let me remind you: favor is not a feeling—it's a force. You may feel pressure, but favor is still active. You may be facing challenges, but you're still covered. You may be in a storm, but the shield has not left you.

So walk boldly. Pray boldly. Dream boldly.

You are not alone.

You are not exposed.

You are not defenseless.

You are surrounded by favor.

Scripture Focus:

"You surround him with favor as with a shield." — Psalm 5:12 (NASB 1995)

Reflection Question:

Where have you been living cautiously that God is

NATE FREEMAN

calling you to walk boldly because of His favor?

Declaration:

I am not afraid of what's ahead—I am surrounded. God's favor shields me, leads me, and fights for me. I walk covered, confident, and called.

◆ ◆ ◆

Conclusion: You're Not Lucky—You're Chosen

If you made it to Chapter 31, that's not just commitment—that's confirmation. Confirmation that deep down, you know you were made for more. You didn't just read about favor—you've been walking through it. One word. One chapter. One moment of clarity at a time.

This wasn't just a devotional. This was a divine reminder. Favor isn't a feeling—it's a force. It doesn't show up because you did everything right. It shows up because God already called you His.

You're not here by chance. The doors that opened, the strength you found, the healing that's begun— those are fingerprints of favor. And the best part? This isn't the end of a 31-day journey. It's the beginning of a life lived under open heaven.

You may have walked through wilderness, setbacks, silence, or storms. But favor stayed. Even when people didn't. Even when you doubted. Even when it looked like nothing was changing—God was still working.

So don't stop here.

Walk into your next assignment knowing you're not empty—you're equipped. You're not average—you're anointed. The same God who brought you through 31 chapters is writing your next one, and it's drenched in promise.

You're not lucky.

You're chosen.

You're favored.

And you're ready.

— Dr. Nate Freeman

ABOUT THE AUTHOR

Nate Freeman

Dr. Nate Freeman is not just a pastor — he's a voice for the resilient, the overlooked, and the called. With a message forged through personal adversity and deep-rooted faith, Nate has inspired hundreds of thousands through social media, books, and live events to step boldly into the favor of God.

A powerful communicator with a heart for the broken and a voice that resonates, Nate weaves scripture with storytelling, real life with revelation. Whether he's writing devotionals, leading First Christian Church, or encouraging his digital community known as the "God Squad," he brings the message home with fire, authenticity, and purpose.

Nate's life is a living testimony of how God's favor doesn't just open doors — it turns battles into platforms and setbacks into stages.

He is the creator of 31 Days of God's Favor, host of

the podcast "Authenticity," and author of multiple devotionals and faith-based books. When he's not writing or preaching, you'll find him mentoring leaders, building online communities, and walking faithfully in his calling.

Nate lives and leads from Steubenville, Ohio — and every word he writes comes from a place of hard-won hope and relentless faith.

BOOKS BY THIS AUTHOR

A Grateful Heart: Daily Devotion For A Thankful Heart

Dive into the transformative journey of 'A Grateful Heart,' a Christian daily devotional that speaks to both the heart and soul. Whether you're a man or a woman, this scripture-based devotional offers 30 days of inspirational reflections, guiding you closer to spiritual growth and understanding. Each entry, crafted with eloquence by Nate Freeman, serves as a beacon of hope and gratitude, making it a perfect devotional for couples looking to grow together in faith. Accompanied by reflection questions, this devotional journal not only feeds the spirit but also encourages introspection and personal growth. Tailored for those seeking a deeper, guided devotional experience, 'A Grateful Heart' ensures every day is infused with prayer, inspiration, and a renewed sense of God's enduring love. Ideal for teens and adults alike, this is a devotional that transcends age, nurturing a prayerful heart brimming with gratitude.

Discover Peace: 30-Day Devotion Of Tried & Tested Scriptures

In the clamor of everyday life, finding peace can often feel like a distant dream. "Discovering Peace: A 30-Day Devotion on Tried and Tested Scripture" is a beacon for those navigating the rough seas of worry and unrest. This devotional offers a daily respite, a moment to draw breath and find calm in the storm through the enduring wisdom of scripture. Each day presents a passage, a reflection, and a prayer, tailored to guide you toward inner tranquility and spiritual reassurance. Whether it's the stress of the uncertain future, the strain of personal trials, or the search for a quiet moment with God, this book is a companion for your journey, promising a peace that is not just fleeting emotion, but a deep-rooted presence in your daily life.

From Gloom To Glory: Finding Joy Through Jesus In The Midst Of Darkness

Discover the Unstoppable Power of Faith and Joy in the Midst of Life's Darkest Moments

In "From Gloom to Glory," author Nate Freeman offers an inspiring, soul-stirring journey through the valleys of despair to the mountaintops of joy and redemption. This book is not just a read; it's an experience, a journey alongside someone who has walked the treacherous paths of life's most daunting challenges and emerged with a message of hope and triumph. Nate's story is a testament to the unyielding strength found in faith in Jesus Christ, a beacon for anyone navigating through their own dark nights.

A Journey From Despair to Hope, From Darkness to Radiant Light

Nate Freeman, a survivor of kidney failure, a conqueror of blindness, and a victor over near-death experiences, shares his extraordinary story of finding joy in Jesus amidst life's most challenging trials. Each page pulsates with raw emotion, deep insight, and spiritual wisdom. "From Gloom to Glory" is more than just a memoir; it's a guide to finding unshakable joy and strength in the promises of God, even when the world around you seems to be crumbling.

A Book That Echoes With Triumph and Hope

Crafted with heart and depth, "From Gloom to Glory" is a must-read for anyone seeking light in the midst of darkness, peace in times of turmoil, and joy in the place of sorrow. Nate's journey is a powerful reminder that you are never alone, that your struggles are not the end, and that with Jesus, there is always a path to glory. Embark on this transformative journey and uncover the joy that awaits you, the joy that outshines the darkest days and leads to a life of purpose and fulfillment in Christ.

A Companion for the Weary, A Beacon for the Lost

Prepare to be moved, inspired, and uplifted. This book is for the weary heart, the seeking soul, and anyone longing for a reminder of God's unfailing grace and enduring love. Let "From Gloom to Glory" be your companion as you navigate the complexities of life, and find the strength to triumph in the face of adversity.

Upon This Rock: The 7 Foundational Pillars For Your Christian Journey

Upon This Rock equips Christians with the tools they need to perform the work of the ministry. The seven pillars covered in this book are salvation, prayer, the Bible, the Church, water baptism, servant leadership, and the tithe. This book is energetic and provides readers with all of the information they need to get started in their spiritual journey.

Made in the USA
Middletown, DE
11 May 2025

75345983R00080